Meldrum Academy

This book must be returned to ~~below~~

Wealth Of Nations

Malaysia

Jen Green

HODDER
Wayland

an imprint of Hodder Children's Books

Wealth Of Nations series includes:

Brazil	**India**
China	**Malaysia**
Egypt	**Vietnam**

Cover: Main photo: The Petronas Towers in Kuala Lumpur.
Inset: Muslim women at a tea shop.

Title page: Mount Kinabulu in Sabah state.

Contents page: A group of children playing in a park.

Malaysia is a simplified and updated version of the title *Malaysia* in
Hodder Wayland's *Economically Developing Countries* series.

Text copyright © 2001 Hodder Wayland
Volume copyright © 2001 Hodder Wayland

Editor: Polly Goodman
Language consultant: Norah Granger, Senior Lecturer in Education Studies,
Department of Education, University of Brighton.

First published in Great Britain in 1996 by Wayland Publishers Ltd. This edition updated
and published in 2001 by Hodder Wayland, an imprint of Hodder Children's Books.

British Library Cataloguing in Publication Data
Green, Jen
    Malaysia. – (Wealth of Nations)
    1. Malaysia – Economic conditions – 20th century – Juvenile literature
    2. Malaysia – Social conditions – 20th century – Juvenile literature
    3. Malaysia – Geography – Juvenile literature
    I.Title
    959.5'054

ISBN 0 7502 3530 6

Printed and bound in Italy by G. Canale C.S.p.A, Turin.

Hodder Children's Books
A division of Hodder Headline Limited
338 Euston Road, London NW1 3BH

Picture acknowledgements
All photographs are by Jim Holmes, except for: Axiom/Martin Stolworthy *Cover, main*;
Allan Flachs 41, 43; Eye Ubiquitous/John Dakes *Cover, inset*; Ole Steen Hansen 3, 4 17.
Illustrations by Peter Bull.

CONTENTS

INTRODUCTION

Malaysia is a country in South-East Asia. It is made up of three regions, Malaya, Sabah and Sarawak.

Malaya is on a long finger of land called the Malay Peninsula. Sabah and Sarawak are 700 kilometres across the South China Sea, in the north of the large island of Borneo. Malaya, Sabah and Sarawak make up the Federation of Malaysia.

During the nineteenth and early twentieth century, Malaysia was ruled by Britain. It became independent in 1963.

Kuala Lumpur is the capital city of Malaysia. ▶

MALAYSIAN NATION

The Malaysian flag has fourteen red-and-white stripes and a star with fourteen points. They stand for the thirteen states of Malaysia, plus the federal government. The crescent represents Islam, which is the main religion.

MALAYSIA FACTS

Population:	22 million
Area:	329,758 square kilometres
Capital city:	Kuala Lumpur
Language:	Malay
Main religion:	Islam

▲ The thirteen states of Malaysia.

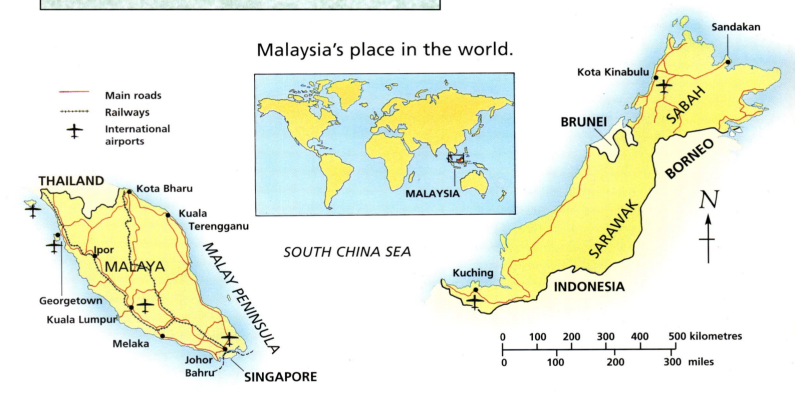

Main roads
Railways
International airports

THAILAND

Kota Bharu

Kuala Terengganu

Ipor

MALAYA

Georgetown

Kuala Lumpur

Melaka

Johor Bahru

SINGAPORE

MALAY PENINSULA

Malaysia's place in the world.

MALAYSIA

SOUTH CHINA SEA

Sandakan

Kota Kinabulu

BRUNEI

SABAH

BORNEO

SARAWAK

Kuching

INDONESIA

N

| 0 | 100 | 200 | 300 | 400 | 500 kilometres |
| 0 | | 100 | | 200 | 300 miles |

Malaysia is a land of contrasts. There are crowded cities, where people live modern lives. But there are also remote rain forests, where people live in more traditional ways. In the countryside, many people are farmers.

Malaysia is developing very quickly. During the 1990s, its economy grew more quickly than any other country in Asia.

Tin, rubber and timber used to be the main goods that were sold abroad. Now manufactured goods such as cars and computer parts are important, too.

QUALITY OF LIFE (1998)	
Life expectancy:	72
% of people over 15 who can read and write:	86%
% of children who go to secondary school:	64%
Children who die under the age of 5: 10 per 1,000	

▼ The city of Kota Kinabalu in Sabah has many modern buildings.

1700s	Europeans, including the British, came to Malaysia as traders. The British made Penang Island, off Malaysia, a British colony.
1919	British Malaya was formed on the Malaysian Peninsula.
1930	Malaysian Communist Party (MCP) formed to fight British rule.
1942	Japanese occupied British Malaya during the Second World War.
1948	MCP struggled to end British rule after the end of the Second World War.
1955	Malaysian political parties called for independence.
1957	Malaya became independent.
1963	Federation of Malaysia was formed from Malaya, Singapore, Sabah and Sarawak.
1965	Singapore left the federation.

A farmer walks home after a hard day's work in the rice fields of West Malaysia. ▶

LAND AND CLIMATE

WEST MALAYSIA

Malaya is the most developed part of Malaysia. A chain of mountains runs down the peninsula, dividing it into west and east.

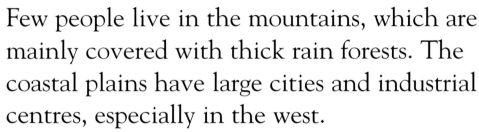

▲ Thick rain forests cover many parts of Malaysia.

Few people live in the mountains, which are mainly covered with thick rain forests. The coastal plains have large cities and industrial centres, especially in the west.

On the western plains, villages are surrounded by rice fields. There are also plantations of rubber and oil palm trees, and tin mines. The eastern strip holds fewer towns and factories. Most people there live by farming or fishing.

▼ This map shows the height of the land in Malaysia. Highland areas are coloured brown. Lowlands are shown in green.

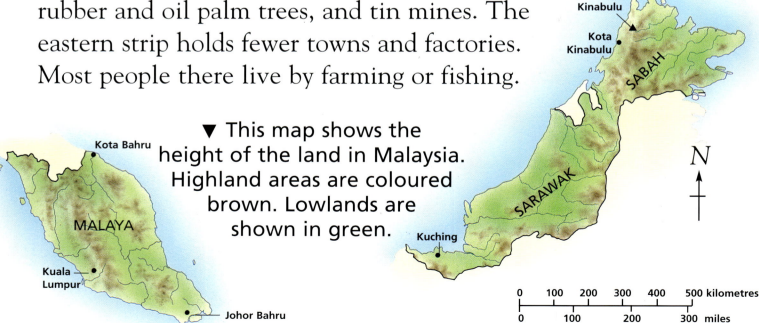

Kota Bahru

MALAYA

Kuala
Lumpur

Johor Bahru

Mount
Kinabulu

Kota
Kinabulu

SABAH

SARAWAK

Kuching

N

| 0 | 100 | 200 | 300 | 400 | 500 kilometres |

| 0 | 100 | 200 | 300 miles |

8

Malaysia is the world's largest exporter of tropical timber. Over half the world's supply of this valuable wood comes from Malaysia. Nearby Indonesia supplies another 27 per cent.

In the past, the local people in Malaysia cut down small areas of forest for farming. Cleared areas were left for a long time so the trees could grow back.

Now logging companies cut down huge areas of forest. They replant the land with fast-growing trees. But the roots of these trees do not protect the soil from being washed away by heavy rain.

'My husband drives a truck that carries logs down to the sawmill. It's a good job and he is well paid. We have our own house in town and all the things we want. But my daughter rarely sees her father because he's away so much.' – Winnie Chan, a logger's wife.

▲ Logging provides a good living for Winnie Chan and her family.

EAST MALAYSIA

In Sabah and Sarawak, coastal plains rise to mountains on the border with Indonesia. Mighty rivers flow down from the mountains across the plains. They include the Rajang river in Sarawak and the Kinabatangan river in Sabah. In some places, the rivers have worn away rocks to make huge caves.

PLANTS AND ANIMALS

Malaysia is home to many kinds of plants and animals. The world's largest flower, called rafflesia, grows in the rain forests of Sabah. Rafflesia flowers measure up to 3 metres across. They give off a bad smell, like rotting meat.

The rain forests are also home to over 200 different kinds of mammals, including monkeys, tigers and leopards. There are also snakes, lizards and colourful butterflies and birds.

In some parts of Malaysia, the forests are disappearing quickly. The giant trees are being cut down for their valuable hardwood, or cleared to make way for farms. When the trees are cut down, forest animals lose their homes. National parks have been set up in some areas to protect the forest.

Sabah and Sarawak are not as developed as Malaya. There are some towns and factories near the coast, but most inland areas are covered by thick rain forests. Most people here are farmers.

◀ The Kinabatangan river in Sabah.

▲ Storm clouds are often seen in Malaysia.

CLIMATE

Malaysia is near the Equator. The climate is tropical, with hot and humid weather all year round. During the day, temperatures often go up to 30 °Celsius. The temperature rarely drops below 20 °Celsius, even at night. Mountains and hilly regions are cooler than the lowlands.

AVERAGE RAINFALL (mm)		
	Kuala Lumpur, Malaya	Labuan, Sabah
Jan–Mar	618	379
April–June	646	993
July–Sept	480	1,032
Oct–Dec	699	1,169
Annual total	2,443	3,573

RAINFALL

Heavy rain falls on all parts of Malaysia. Usually, rain falls on 150–200 days each year, but it does not often last all day.

▲ Clouds gather around the summit of Mount Kinabalu in Sabah.

Seasonal winds called monsoons bring heavy rain at certain times of year. They blow in from the ocean, full of moisture. Later the moisture falls as rain.

In Malaya, the rain is heaviest from September to February. In Sarawak and Sabah, the rainy season lasts for about nine months of the year. Flooding often happens when the rivers burst their banks.

▼ Logging trucks carry trees that have been cut down.

Malaysia's heavy rainfall has allowed rain forests to grow. Some of the oldest forests in the world are in Malaysia.

Malaysia's national parks help to protect the country's scenery and wildlife. The largest park, the Taman Negara National Park, was set up in 1935. It covers 4,300 square kilometres of forest land on the Malay Peninsula. In 1988, a new park, the Endau Rompin National Park, was made to protect another 930 square kilometres of forest.

In Sabah, Malaysia's highest mountain, Mount Kinabalu, is in the middle of another national park. The mountain rises to 4,094 metres. It is one of the highest peaks in South-East Asia. Over 1,000 types of orchids grow in the forests on the slopes, along with rafflesia flowers.

Yassan Sekambeng is a park guide. He works to protect Malaysia's wildlife.▼

'My parents used to believe that the mountain had a spirit, and that we would go there when we died. Now I earn my living here. All the guides and porters who work on Kinabalu respect the wildlife and the forest. We help tourists to understand why we must protect these special places.' – Yassan Sekambeng, a guide on Mount Kinabalu.

TRANSPORT

Good transport is important in any country. In Malaysia, people use roads, railways, aeroplanes and boats to get about.

ROADS

Malaysia's first roads were built when the country was a British colony. Many roads began as tracks to forests, plantations or tin mines. Now these roads have been improved and linked together. Good roads help remote regions to develop.

▲ There are often traffic jams during rush hour in Kuala Lumpur and other big cities.

◄ A road worker repairs a drain next to a modern city road.

Throughout Malaysia, mountains make road transport difficult. Malaya has the best roads. Here, major highways run north to south along the lowlands in the east and west. There are only a few places where paved roads cross the central mountains.

In Sabah and Sarawak, the roads are not so good. Until about 1985, Sabah's roads were mostly dirt tracks. Now, roads between the major towns are paved.

The main north-south highway in Malaya is a dual carriageway for most of the way. ▼

In Kuala Lumpur, the roads get very busy during the rush hours. To help the traffic, a new railway line called the Light Rail Transit System (LRT) was built to link the city centre with the suburbs. It opened in 1995. The line has electric trains.

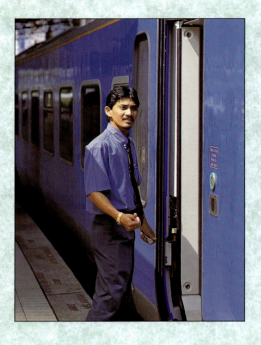

▲ A train operator prepares to board one of the new trains.

All journeys were free for the first few days after the new line opened, so everyone could get to know the system. Now people have to pay, but many people still use the LRT because it is comfortable and quick.

In the busy city centre, the new railway line has been built above the roads. ▼

'The new electric trains have made life easier in Kuala Lumpur. The roads are so busy these days, and parking is expensive in the city. Now many people travel to work by train and leave their cars at home.'
– LRT train operator.

RAILWAYS

Malaysia's railways also date back to colonial times (see the map on page 5). The main railway line runs north to south through the western plain of Malaya. Another line links the towns of the eastern coastal strip with Kuala Lumpur in the west.

AIR TRAVEL

Air travel allows people to get to remote parts of Malaysia quickly. The national air company, Malaysia Airlines, runs daily flights between most large towns in Sabah, Sarawak and Malaya.

A Malaysia Airlines plane. ▼

AIRPORTS

International airports in Malaya link Malaysia with the rest of the world. Even small towns have their own airstrips.

WATER TRAVEL

Water transport is another important type of travel. Ships take goods and passengers between ports in Malaya, Sarawak, Sabah and beyond.

In remote parts of Sarawak, the rivers are also used for transport. Fast boats carry goods and passengers between river towns and villages.

▲ This fast boat takes goods and passengers between river ports in Sarawak.

THE PEOPLES OF MALAYSIA

Malaysia's population is made up of many different peoples. Malays are the largest group. There are also many Chinese, Indians, and peoples who have lived in Malaysia for hundreds of years.

This mix has come about because of Malaysia's history. In the past, the country was on trade routes between India and China.

The different peoples of Malaysia speak various languages and have different religions and customs. There are sometimes problems between Malays, the largest group, and Chinese people, who own most of the businesses.

Newspapers are printed in many different languages, including Malay, Chinese, and English. ▼

About half of all Malaysian people live in the countryside. This is different from most countries today, where most people live in cities.

In the countryside, most people work as farmers. Some live in small villages called kampungs, in thatched houses built on stilts.

Since the 1950s, many people have moved to the cities from the countryside. Recently, the government has helped new towns to grow, so the big cities do not get too crowded.

Malay men praying in a mosque. Islam is the main religion in Malaysia. ▼

MALAYS

Malays make up about half of Malaysia's population. Most live in Malaya.

Malays are Muslims and have their own culture. Malay is also the country's official language. This is the language that children are taught in school.

◄ An Indian shopkeeper shows the fine cloth she sells.

ETHNIC GROUPS AND RELIGIONS	
Ethnic groups	
Malay	50%
Chinese	35%
Indian	10%
Local peoples	5%
Religions	
Islam	50%
Chinese faiths	25%
Hindu	7%
Buddhist	6%
Christian	6%
Other	6%

CHINESE

Chinese people make up about 35 per cent of Malaysia's population. Many came to Malaysia in the nineteenth century. Most speak Chinese, and they have their own religions, including Buddhism. Chinese people run most of the country's businesses, so they have a lot of power.

INDIANS

About 10 per cent of Malaysians are Indian. In the early twentieth century, many came to work in the plantations, which were then owned by the British.

LOCAL PEOPLES

Local peoples, mainly from Sabah and Sarawak, are only a small percentage of Malaysia's population. In Malaya, local groups are known as Orang Asli, which means 'the original people'. They mainly live in the mountains, where they grow crops or gather forest fruits.

▲ Many houses are built on stilts in Sabah.

THE IBAN OF SARAWAK

The Iban are people from Sarawak. In the past, the Iban and other local groups had little contact with the outside world. They lived in the rain forest, where they gathered food such as roots and grew rice.

Now the Ibans' traditional way of life is being destroyed. The rain forests where they have lived for centuries are being cut down for timber. The streams and rivers that water their lands are being used to make hydroelectric power.

Forced off their lands, some Iban people have moved to large towns in Sarawak, such as Sibu. They go in search of work so they can earn a living, instead of living off the land. Other Ibans visit the towns to find tourists who want to visit their homes and stay in one of their traditional longhouses.

In Sabah and Sarawak, the largest local groups are the Dayaks and Kadazan peoples. Many live in large dwellings called longhouses, which are often built on stilts on the banks of rivers. The stilts protect the house from flooding when the river rises after heavy rain. Some local people live as farmers. Others hunt and gather forest fruits. Local groups suffer when the forests are cut down.

▲ An Iban man outside his longhouse.

Tourists now bring money to Iban groups who still live in traditional ways.

For the Iban and other local groups who still live in remote regions, signs of change are everywhere. Longhouses are still built using traditional methods. But many now have goods from the developed world, such as televisions and radios.

'We Iban still live in longhouses. Sharing one building helps us to stay together as a group. The longhouse we live in now is new because we had to move away from our valley. The place where we used to live is now underwater, since they built the new hydroelectric dam.' – Nyambar Nyelang, from Sibu.

FARMING AND NATURAL RESOURCES

Malaysia has many natural resources that have helped it to develop. Farming, forestry, mining and energy production are all important to the country's economy.

Forest land is cleared to make way for a large plantation. ▼

AGRICULTURE

Farming was once the main source of Malaysia's wealth. But as manufacturing and mining have grown, it has become less important. Until recently, one in every three workers in Malaysia worked in farming. Now the figure is only one in five.

NATURAL RESOURCES, 1998	
Production (in millions of ringgit)	
Palm oil	4,644
Rubber	1,688
Livestock, forestry and fishing	11,081
Mining and quarrying	14,425

Malaysia's main farm products are oil from oil palm trees, rubber, cocoa and rice. Other crops are pineapples, coconuts, pepper and tobacco. Hardwood cut from Malaysia's forests also brings in cash from abroad.

▲ Oil palm plantations such as this one cover huge areas in Malaysia.

RUBBER, PALM OIL AND COCOA

Malaysia is one of the world's biggest producers of rubber. The bark of the rubber tree makes a sap called latex, which is turned into rubber. Rubber trees did not grow naturally in Malaysia. The British brought them from Brazil during the 1880s. Now rubber plantations are seen all over Malaysia.

FARMING IN MALAYSIA

Over the last thirty years, farming has become less important in Malaysia. This is because recent government policies have harmed farming methods.

From the 1970s, the Malaysian government favoured poor Malay farmers, who owned small plots of land, rather than owners of large plantations. The government encouraged farmers to grow 'cash crops' to sell abroad, such as rubber, oil palm and cocoa, rather than crops to feed their families.

Palm fruit arrives at a mill to be crushed. ▼

Until recently, Malaysia was the world's top rubber producer. But lately, it has been overtaken by Thailand and Indonesia. Rubber can now be produced more cheaply in these countries because workers' wages are lower and machinery is cheaper.

In fact, cash crops are best grown by owners of large plantations, who can afford specialist machinery and fertilizers. The government's policy meant that the land was not farmed in the best way.

Many small farmers could not earn a living growing cash crops. In the end, some had to leave their land and go to the cities to look for work.

▲ A plantation manager checks newly harvested palm fruit.

Palm oil has been Malaysia's most important crop since the 1980s. The oil is taken from the fruit of the palm tree. Cocoa is a fairly new crop in Malaysia. It has only been grown since the 1950s, but now the country is a big producer.

This tin mine has been closed for years. It has become overgrown with grass and plants. ▶

MINERALS

Malaysia has large deposits of tin. Tin mining was once the country's biggest industry.

During the early 1980s, more than 60,000 tonnes of tin came from Malaysia's mines each year. But ten years later, only 10,000 tonnes were being mined. The market price of tin had fallen, which meant that it was not worth mining any more.

ENERGY

Malaysia has the natural resources to supply all the energy it needs. Large oil and gas fields lie off the east coast of the Malay Peninsula and in Sarawak and Sabah.

Hydroelectric power is also becoming important. It is generated from fast-flowing rivers. In recent years, Malaysia's industries have grown and the demand for electricity has increased.

'I come from a family of miners. My father came here from Thailand to work in the mines in about 1888. I worked in the local mine from a young age. But in the 1950s all the tin mines in our area closed.' – Mr Lim-Chene Hoon, a former tin miner (left).

OIL MINING AT KERTEH

The port of Kerteh, on the east coast of Malaya, was once a peaceful fishing village. Then oil was discovered offshore. Petronas, the state oil and gas company, moved in to mine the valuable oil.

Industrial buildings sprang up, along with new estates to house the oil workers. Kerteh has been changed, despite many local people's wish to carry on with their traditional way of life.

In 1992, the government sold off parts of TNB, the national electricity board, to pay for schemes to produce more energy.

Now the state oil and gas company, Petronas, sells its gas to private power stations. They supply the country with electricity through a network of power lines called the national grid.

THE BAKUN DAM

Malaysia has planned several new hydroelectric schemes to help meet the country's energy needs. But many people do not like the plans because they mean making reservoirs that flood huge areas of land.

The Bakun Dam is a large hydroelectric scheme. It is planned for the Rajang river in Sarawak. Work on the dam in the middle of the rain forest began in the late 1990s. When complete, the dam will flood 700 square kilometres of rain forest. About 6,000 people will have to move and settle elsewhere.

The scheme has caused many arguments since it was suggested in the 1980s. Planners say the dam will produce energy for Malaysia's growing industries. Some local people support the project because it will bring new jobs and roads to the area. Conservationists, who fight to protect the natural world, argue that it will cause too much damage. Some would prefer a few small dams rather than one giant dam.

This small dam in Sarawak has flooded the area behind it. The Bakun Dam would flood a much larger area of forest. ▶

GROWING INDUSTRIES

Malaysia has one of the world's fastest-growing economies. Farming and mining are important, but manufacturing is growing the fastest.

Between the 1970s and 2000, Malaysia's manufacturing overtook tin and rubber production as the country's main earner.

▲ These new factories are almost finished.

MALAYSIA'S ECONOMY, 1999	
	Percentage of GDP
Manufacturing	29%
Farming	9%
Trade and hotels	15%
Banking and finance	12%
Mining	7%
Transport and communications	8%
Other	20%

◄ These cars made in Malaysia will be sold abroad.

PENANG: 'SILICON ISLAND'

Business is booming on the island of Penang, off the north-west coast of Malaya. During the 1960s, many people on the island were out of work. The Penang authorities encouraged foreign businesses to come and set up factories on the island.

By the 1990s, almost everyone had a job. But few workers were skilled and wages were low.

Recently, Penang has become a centre for the electronics industry. There are so many hi-tech factories that it is now called 'Silicon Island'. Penang specializes in making computer disk drives. The island is joined to the mainland by the Penang Bridge, Asia's longest road bridge.

Top international companies are now based in Penang.

'I grew up on Sarawak, but went to Malaya for training. I was trained as a technician by an American company which is going to build a new factory near my home town. With my new skills, I feel I can move forward in the future.' – Edward Philip Ak Aga, a computer technician, aged 23.

Many of the factories are owned by Japanese or American companies, but this is changing. With the help of training programmes, skilled local workers are now helping businesses owned by Malaysians.

A branch of one of Malaysia's banks. ▼

MANUFACTURING

Malaysia's factories produce computer equipment, steel, plastics, chemicals and cloth. The country is now one of the world's top makers of computer disk drives.

Malaysia's car industry is another big success story. It produces tens of thousands of cars for sale, both at home and abroad.

In the past, many factories in Malaysia were owned by foreign companies. The profits went abroad, rather than being spent at home. As the country develops further, a larger number of companies will be owned by Malaysians themselves.

◄ Edward Philip Ak Aga shows the tools of his trade.

FINANCE

Malaysia is also an important centre for banking and finance. This area of the economy was affected when South-East Asia was hit by economic troubles between 1996 and 1997.

In Malaysia, there are not enough skilled people to fill all the jobs. Recently the government has taken steps to try to change this.

In the past, more Malaysian students studied arts subjects rather than science at university. This was because science is not easy to teach in Malay, the country's language, which is the language taught in schools.

Science is much easier to learn in English. In recent years, Chinese Malaysians have found it easier to get technical training than Malays. This is because many Chinese students go to colleges abroad and study in English. Recently, some people have suggested that Malaysian schools should teach in English, to tackle this problem.

BUILDING

In recent years there has been a great deal of new building in Malaysia. New housing estates have been built in the suburbs of Kuala Lumpur and other big cities.

A builder lifts a bag of cement, which is scarce in Malaysia. ▶

The building work has caused a shortage of building supplies such as cement. The government now carefully controls cement prices and supplies to stop it from running out.

Rubbish fills a sewer in Kuala Lumpur. ▶

POLLUTION

As the number of factories in Malaysia grows, so does the amount of pollution.

In 1994, a smoky haze covered Malaysia. It trapped car exhaust gases and factory fumes close to the ground. People stayed inside their homes and schools were closed. Fires on the nearby islands of Indonesia were blamed for the haze.

The following year, the haze came again. Only this time, there were no fires to blame. Some people in cities feel they would rather do without all the new factories if they bring pollution.

◀ Workers in front of Petronas Towers. The world's tallest building stands 452 metres high.

'We are very proud to be working on this project. Engineers from Japan and South Korea helped us build the towers. They had the technology to help us, but now we have it too.' – Mr Ifmail and Mr Mohamad, who are builders.

THE PROTON CAR

Malaysia was one of the first countries in South-East Asia to make its own model of car. In 1985, the national car company made the Proton Saga car. The Japananese car company, Mitsubishi, helped.

Ten years later, 70 per cent of the cars bought in Malaysia were Protons. The car has also been very successful overseas. In 1994, Malaysia brought out a second, cheaper car, called the Kancil.

Workers assemble cars in a factory. ▼

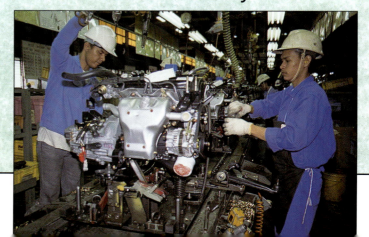

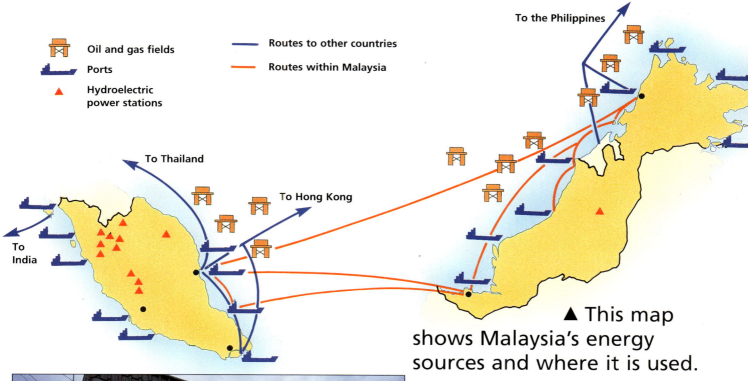

Key:

- 🏭 Oil and gas fields
- ⚓ Ports
- 🔺 Hydroelectric power stations
- Routes to other countries
- Routes within Malaysia

To the Philippines

To Thailand

To Hong Kong

To India

▲ This map shows Malaysia's energy sources and where it is used.

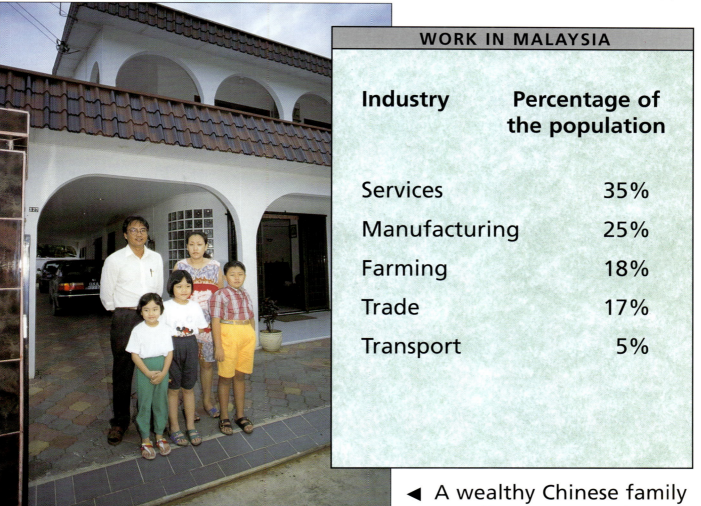

WORK IN MALAYSIA	
Industry	**Percentage of the population**
Services	35%
Manufacturing	25%
Farming	18%
Trade	17%
Transport	5%

◄ A wealthy Chinese family show off their home.

TOURISM AND LEISURE

Malaysia is a popular place for people to spend their holidays. Tourists from many countries come to relax on the white sandy beaches and swim in the clear seas.

Hikers and other holiday-makers visit mountains and hilly regions such as the Cameron Highlands. Rainforest parks and reserves attract tourists as well as protecting the local wildlife.

Tourists try new sports on Malaysia's beaches, or just enjoy the sunshine. ▶

Tourists relax by the pool at a luxury hotel in Penang. ▼

Some tourists stay in the longhouses of the Iban. There they see traditional ways of life. Malaysia's luxury hotels are good places to hold business meetings.

In 1990, 1994 and 1998, the government encouraged foreign tourists with special 'Visit Malaysia' years. In 1998, the country hosted the Commonwealth Games.

'There is so much to see in Malaysia. Everyone is so friendly.' – Marion Esch, a German tourist (left).

The Eastern and Oriental Express is a luxury train service. It runs through Malaya on its way from Bangkok in Thailand to Singapore. Inside, the train is fitted out in the style of the 1930s. Both Western tourists and wealthy Asians enjoy riding the train.

▲ Luxury hotels in Malaysia are built to encourage Western tourists.

▲ A Malaysian family visits the local zoo.

LOCAL TOURISTS

Malaysian people also enjoy their country's beaches and other attractions. People who live in the cities enjoy the peace of the countryside on their holidays. Good jobs in the city give them more money to spend in their leisure time.

LEISURE

In their time off, people enjoy a mixture of traditional Malaysian and Western pastimes. Young people play video games, watch American films or meet in hamburger bars. Badminton, soccer, hockey, golf and tennis are popular Western sports.

Sepak raga is a traditional Malaysian sport that is a cross between soccer and volley-ball. Players kick and head the ball to stop it touching the ground. Kite-flying and top-spinning are also traditional pastimes.

TOURISM IN SABAH

Tourism in eastern Sabah is not well developed. Most of the resorts there have been built to suit rich tourists from abroad. Local people and poorer tourists complain they cannot afford to visit.

Uncle Tan runs a different sort of guesthouse near the port of Sandakan. He offers tourists the chance to visit tropical islands and rainforest camps quite cheaply.

'There are many different sorts of tourists, but everyone wants to see the real Sabah. We must try to suit everyone, and at the same time, protect the natural world.' – Uncle Tan, the owner of a small guesthouse.

◀ Uncle Tan runs a guesthouse in Sabah.

▲ Langkawi Island, off the Malay Peninsula, has beautiful beaches.

PALAU LABUAN

The island of Palau Labuan is just off the coast of Sabah. It is an unusual place. The island is a small, quiet tourist resort and also a centre for shopping and finance. People go there to shop because the goods are duty-free.

Palua Labuan is not yet well developed. There are few skyscrapers, luxury hotels, or tourist attractions. But all this may change soon. The government plans to make the island into a luxury resort and banking centre. A new financial area is being built.

THE FUTURE

Malaysia has one of the fastest-growing economies in the world. But poverty is still a problem in both the countryside and the cities. Some Malaysians are very wealthy, but others are very poor.

In 1990, the Malaysian government announced an important plan for the country's future. The aim is for Malaysia to become a fully developed industrial country by the year 2020. The government calls its plan 'Vision 2020'. The idea appears on posters and banners everywhere.

Malaysia's plans include many large building projects. New housing estates and factories are being built in the big cities. A new international airport has been opened at Sepang near Kuala Lumpur. A new 'megacity' called Putrajaya is planned 40 kilometres south of the capital.

▲ This new port in Sabah is being built on land reclaimed from the sea.

▲ A poster advertises the new international airport at Sepang.

44

'Kuala Lumpur is changing fast. We are building whole new districts with shops, which will be like new small towns.'
– Joseph Khaw, an architect.

Planners must take care that all this new development does not spoil the countryside or cause too much pollution.

Unlike many developing nations, Malaysia has quite a small population. This causes problems when there are not enough people to fill all the jobs.

Workers are needed to help the economy grow. Without enough people to take all the new jobs, Malaysia's fast economic growth will slow down.

During the 1990s, Malaysia's economy grew so fast that it is now a newly industrialized nation. In future, the government must manage development carefully to continue the country's success.

▲ Architects help to shape the future in Malaysia.

GLOSSARY

Cash crop A crop that is grown for sale, not to provide food for the farmer.

Colony A country that is ruled by another country.

Crop A plant such as wheat or rice, that is specially grown to be harvested.

Duty-free Not taxed.

Economy The wealth and resources belonging to a country.

Export To sell goods abroad.

Exporter A country that sells goods abroad.

Federal government A central government that handles the common affairs of different states while the states keep separate control of their own local affairs.

Fertilizer A chemical added to the soil to make it produce better crops.

Gross Domestic Product (GDP) The value of all the goods and services made in a country during one year.

Humid Slightly wet.

Hydroelectricity Energy that is produced by harnessing the power of fast-flowing water.

Independence Free from foreign rule.

Industrialize When a country grows industries based on machines.

Invest To put money into a business or product so it will make more money.

Irrigate To water crops using channels or pipes.

Manufacturing Making natural products into goods that can be sold.

Monsoon A wind that blows in tropical regions at certain times of year, and sometimes brings heavy rain.

Peninsula A piece of land that extends far out into the water.

Plantation A large farm that produces a single crop such as sugar, cocoa or rubber.

Population The people living in a place or country.

Reclaimed land An area that was once underwater, but has been drained.

Resource A supply such as oil or water that people need.

Ringgit The currency, or money, used in Malaysia.

Tropical Belonging to the Tropics, the zone on either side of the Equator, between the Tropics of Cancer and Capricorn.

TOPIC WEB

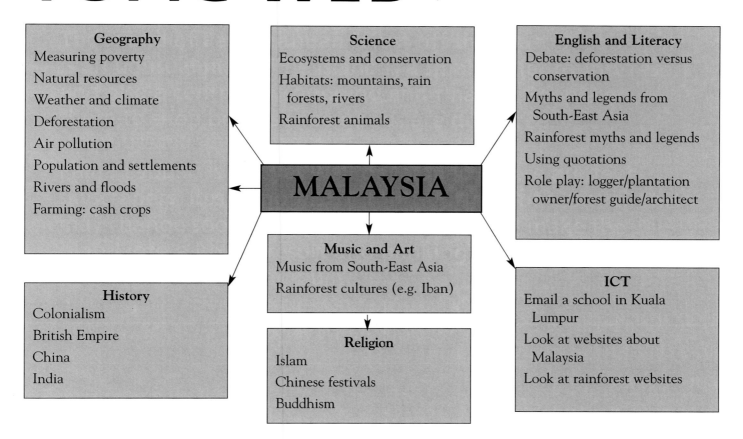

Geography
Measuring poverty
Natural resources
Weather and climate
Deforestation
Air pollution
Population and settlements
Rivers and floods
Farming: cash crops

Science
Ecosystems and conservation
Habitats: mountains, rain forests, rivers
Rainforest animals

English and Literacy
Debate: deforestation versus conservation
Myths and legends from South-East Asia
Rainforest myths and legends
Using quotations
Role play: logger/plantation owner/forest guide/architect

MALAYSIA

History
Colonialism
British Empire
China
India

Music and Art
Music from South-East Asia
Rainforest cultures (e.g. Iban)

Religion
Islam
Chinese festivals
Buddhism

ICT
Email a school in Kuala Lumpur
Look at websites about Malaysia
Look at rainforest websites

FINDING OUT MORE

BOOKS TO READ
Continents: Asia by David Lambert
(Hodder Wayland, 1997)
Discovering Malaysia by Richard Balkwill
(Zoë Books, 1997)
Real World: South-East Asia by Anita Ganeri
(Watts, 1995)

ADDRESSES AND WEBSITES
Asia Observer – Vietnam
www.asiaobserver.com/malaysia.htm
News and background information on Malaysia.

Lonely Planet – Destination Malaysia
www.lonelyplanet.com/destinations/south_east_
asia/malaysia/   Good web pages on Malaysia.

Malaysia Tourism Promotion Board
57, Trafalgar Square, London WC2
www.interknowledge.com/malaysia/
Background information about Malaysia,
including a visit to a longhouse in Borneo.

Malaysian High Commission
45 Belgravia Square, London SW1X 82J
The information library can provide facts about
Malaysia, including a booklet, *Malaysia in Brief*.
Tel: 020 7919 0264

INDEX

Page numbers in **bold** show photographs or illustrations.